Fill-in-the-Blank Stories

WORD FAMILIES

50 Cloze-Format Practice Pages That Target and Teach the Top 50 Word Families

by Linda B. Ross

New York • Toronto • London • Auckland • Sydney
Mexico City • New Delhi • Hong Kong • Buenos Aires

Teaching Resources

Editor: Joan Novelli
Cover design by Jason Robinson
Interior design by Holly Grundon
Cover and interior illustrations by Bari Weissman

ISBN-13: 978-0-439-45861-0
ISBN-10: 0-439-45861-7
Copyright © 2008 by Linda B. Ross
All rights reserved.
Printed in the U.S.A.

2 3 4 5 6 7 8 9 10 40 15 14 13 12 11 10 09 08

Contents

Introduction

This book features 50 engaging stories that provide structured practice for learning 55 key phonograms. Experts agree that early instruction with word families helps children develop reading fluency. When children learn to recognize the letter (or series of letters) that stands for a particular sound or series of sounds, they can apply this knowledge to decode new words quickly and efficiently. The story pages in this book provide the repeated practice children need to master these skills, helping them strengthen their knowledge of word parts, deepen their bank of decoding strategies, and become stronger readers.

What the Research Says

As noted in *Phonics From* A *to* Z by Wiley Blevins (Scholastic, 2006), "phonograms are reliable and generalizable. Of the 286 phonograms that appeared in the primary-level text reviewed in one classic study, 272 (95%) were pronounced the same in every word in which they were found (Durrell, 1963). In addition, these 272 reliable phonograms can be found in 1,437 of the words common to the speaking vocabularies of primary-age children (Murphy, 1957)."

About Phonograms

A phonogram is a letter or group of letters that stands for a sound or series of sounds. The phonogram *-ay* in *day* has two letters and stands for one sound— long *a*. The phonogram *-un* in *fun* stands for two sounds—(/u/ /n/). Words that end in the same phonogram belong to the same "word family." The words *day*, *say*, and *play* are all part of the -*ay* word family. The words *fun*, *sun*, and *run* belong to the -*un* word family.

What's Inside?

From three sleepy sheep to a new puppy named Max, the characters in these charming stories will bring children back again and again to build essential reading skills. Each student page follows a format that children will quickly learn to recognize, thus allowing them to focus their energies on learning and using the words rather than figuring out what to do. Here's a look at the components for each page.

Word Family: The heading at the top of each story page identifies the target phonogram(s). Most stories target one word family. Several focus on two.

Fill-In Story: A cloze format invites children to fill in words to complete each story. Stories are carefully structured to meet the needs of early readers.

Word Bank: This list provides students with all the word choices they need to complete the story.

Illustration: An illustration accompanies each story, and supports early readers in understanding the text.

Word Search: This puzzle invites children to locate the target story words, reinforcing word recognition skills and building vocabulary.

Teaching With the Stories

You can use the stories in any order that best supports your goals for whole-class, small-group, and individual instruction. Model for children how to complete a page before having them do so on their own.

1. Display a story page so all children can see it (for example, by using an overhead).

2. Read the directions aloud, and then direct children's attention to the Word Bank. Point to each word in order as you read it. Think aloud about words that end with the same sound (for most stories, this will be all of the words).

3. Direct children's attention to the title of the story. Read aloud the title, again noticing words that end with the same sound. You might take a moment to notice the illustration, and think aloud about what the story might be about.

4. As you read the story, model concepts of print, including where to begin, going from left to right, and the return sweep to the next line. Pause at each blank to think aloud about which word belongs in the blank. (It may be helpful for children to read on past a blank to finish a sentence, as the end of the sentence might provide clues to the missing word.) This is a good opportunity to teach strategies for figuring out the correct word choice, including through context. For example, in "At the Vet" (page 39) the first blank in the story follows the words "Dennis has a dog named ____." You might point out that you know names begin with a capital letter. That leads you to the word *Jet* in the Word Bank. Write in the word, and continue. (As another strategy, you might show children how to lightly draw a line through each word in the Word Bank as they use it.)

5. When you have filled in all of the blanks, read the story, modeling characteristics of fluency, such as using appropriate expression and pausing at punctuation.

6. Complete the Word Search, showing children how to look across, down, and diagonally—but not backward—for the words in the Word Bank. Place a check next to each word as you find it. Once you find all of the words, read them aloud.

Teaching Tip

After modeling how to use a story page, you might invite students to take turns at the overhead, modeling for you how to complete the same page (use a fresh copy). This will encourage independence as they complete story pages on their own.

Connections to the Language Arts Standards

The story pages and extension activities in this book are designed to support you in meeting the following standards as outlined by Mid-continent Research for Education and Learning (McREL), an organization that collects and synthesizes national and state curriculum standards—and proposes what teachers should provide for their students to become proficient in language arts, among other curriculum areas.

Teaching Tip

The activity pages in this book also support components of the Reading First program (U.S. Department of Education): phonemic awareness, phonics, vocabulary development, reading fluency, and reading comprehension strategies.

Reading

- Understands how print is organized and read
- Uses mental images based on pictures and print to aid in comprehension of text
- Uses meaning clues to aid comprehension and make predictions
- Uses phonetic and structural analysis to decode unknown words
- Understands level-appropriate sight words and vocabulary
- Knows main ideas or theme, setting, main characters, main events, sequence, and problems in stories
- Summarizes information found in texts (retells in own words)
- Makes simple inferences regarding the order of events and possible outcomes
- Relates stories to personal experiences

Source: *Content Knowledge: A Compendium of Standards and Benchmarks for K–12 Education* (4th ed.). Mid-continent Research for Education and Learning, 2004.

Classroom Management Tips

Whether you photocopy each story page at the time of use, or prepare class sets of the stories in advance, a simple storage system will make it easy to build a collection that you can keep on hand for later use or repeated practice.

- Place each set of stories in a file folder. Tape or glue a sample page to the front for reference, or label the tab with the target phonogram(s) and title.
- To encourage self-checking, create an answer key, filling in the words to each story and circling the words in the word search. Attach to the back of the envelope or file folder. Or, place answer keys in a binder. (For a complete set of answers, see pages 10–14.)

Activities to Use With Any Story

The activities here extend what students learn with the story pages. You'll find activities that reinforce rhyming skills, before and after reading

Word Wall Builders

Extend learning by creating word walls or charts based on target words from the stories.

1. Copy target words from a story on chart paper or a whiteboard.

2. Read the words with children and invite them to suggest other words that rhyme. Record their ideas on the chart paper.

3. Circle the words from the story, and then ask children what other words you should circle. Explain that all of the words you circle need to belong to the same word family.

4. Circle words with the same phonogram, and discuss with children any words that don't belong. For example, if you are focusing on the phonogram -*ide* and a child suggests the word *cried*, take a moment to notice that the word *cried* rhymes with the -*ide* words, but has a different spelling pattern.

5. Copy all of the words with the same phonogram on large index cards or sheets of paper. Create pictures to go with words from the story (or enlarge the illustration from the story page) to provide a visual reminder. Display pictures and words as a word wall. Use removable adhesive to create a portable word wall that children can take to their desk and then return to the wall when finished.

Pocket Chart Practice

The short stories in this book lend themselves well to pocket chart activities. Suggestions for creating these activities follow.

Who Has the Word? Write each line of a story on a sentence strip, leaving spaces for the target words as indicated. Cut sentence strips to fit the spaces and write a target word on each. Hand out the word cards to different children. In the pocket chart, place sentence strips in order. Read aloud the story. When you come to a missing word ask, "Who has the word that goes here?" Have that child place the word in the correct space. Continue in this way to complete the story, and then read it aloud together.

Scrambled Stories: Write each sentence of a story on a sentence strip, filling in any missing words. Mix up the strips and place them in a pocket chart. Invite children to help you sequence the sentences to unscramble the story. Number the backs of the sentence strips so children can work independently or in pairs to place the sentences in order, and then check their work. As a variation, cut apart sentences into individual words. Challenge children to arrange the words in order.

Teaching Tip

You can also use the pocket chart stories to focus on a new set of words, such as sight words. To do this, fill in the original target words when writing the story on sentence strips and leave blanks for a new set of target words. Write the missing words on sentence strips trimmed to size and let children use them to complete the story.

Story Hunt

Use any story for an interactive experience that encourages children to take a closer look at the text.

1. Copy a story on chart paper, leaving spaces for the missing words. Copy the word bank to the side.

2. Have children help you fill in the missing words, and then read the story together.

3. Then invite children to take turns hunting for something in the story, using a highlighter to mark it when they find it. For example, you might ask a child to find two words that begin with *th* or a sentence that ends with "!" (and then discuss why this punctuation mark was used). Children can locate rhyming words (for example, find two words that rhyme with *say*), hunt for commas, or highlight words that name people, places, and things, as well as action words. The possibilities are endless.

Encouraging Comprehension

The stories in this book are short, but provide many opportunities to practice comprehension strategies. After children complete a story, revisit it together. Ask questions to help children explore their understanding of the story. For example, after reading "Slide Down!" (page 42), ask:

- Who is this story about? (*Penny and Pilar*)

- What do they like to do together? (*ride their bikes, play hide-and-seek, play on the slide*)

- What problem are they having? (*they can't fit on the slide together*)

- How do you think they'll solve this problem? (*take turns*)

Follow up by inviting children to retell the story in their own words.

Fluency Practice

The brevity of the stories makes them just right for fluency practice.

1. Copy a story on chart paper. Have children help you fill in the missing words.

2. Read the story aloud, modeling good reading behaviors for pacing, expression, punctuation, and inflection. For example, use stories with more than one character (and dialogue) to model how to use a different voice for each character. Model how question marks and exclamation points give you clues about expression.

3. Read the story together, using an echo reading approach. You read one line, and children repeat it, echoing your pacing, phrasing, and intonation.

4. Read the story as a group, again encouraging children to follow along with pacing, phrasing, and intonation.

Story Switcheroo

Have some fun with the stories, using the characters, settings, and events to create new stories.

1. Write characters' names on slips of paper. Place them in a bag and label it "Characters." Do the same with story settings (such as "the kitchen"), events (such as "raking leaves"), and "problems" (such as "having a cold").

2. Let children take turns choosing a slip from each bag. Use the elements to tell a new story. Write it on chart paper and let children illustrate to create a new set of stories to read.

Answer Key

Page 15
The Big Race

Answers:
Grace, race, face, pace, place

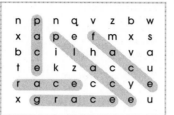

Page 20
A Cap for Dale

Answers:
whale, Dale, sale, pale, tale

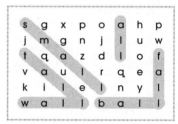

Page 16
Quack! Quack!

Answers:
Jack, back, quack, sack, snack

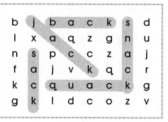

Page 21
A Fall Day

Answers:
fall, tall, All, small, ball, wall

Page 17
Sail Away!

Answers:
Gail, mail, sail, pail, tail

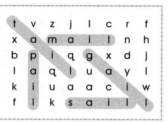

Page 22
I Am Sam

Answers:
Sam, am, Pam, jam, swam, Gram

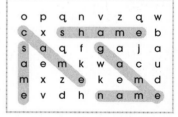

Page 18
A Train to Grandpa's House

Answers:
Jane, train, rain, lane, plane

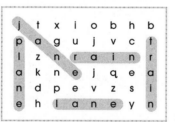

Page 23
It's a Shame!

Answers:
came, name, same, game, shame

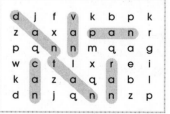

Page 19
Birthday Cake

Answers:
cake, Jake, bake, take, shake, Wake

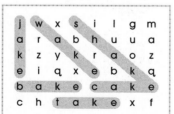

Page 24
In the Van

Answers:
van, Can, Dan, pan, ran, tan

Page 25
A Grand Day

Answers:
hand, sand, land,
band, stand, grand

Word Search Answers:

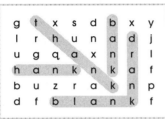

Page 30
A Date to Skate

Answers:
Kate, skate, gate,
late, date, hate

Word Search Answers:

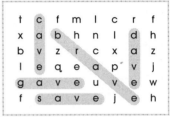

Page 26
A Trip to the Bank

Answers:
bank, Hank, drank,
blank, thank

Word Search Answers:

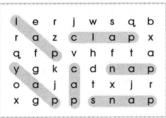

Page 31
Brave Dave

Answers:
Dave, cave, save,
brave, gave

Word Search Answers:

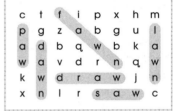

Page 27
Snap and Clap

Answers:
cap, snap, clap,
yap, nap, lap

Word Search Answers:

Page 32
A Fawn on the Lawn

Answers:
dawn, paw, saw,
fawn, lawn, draw

Word Search Answers:

Page 28
Crash!

Answers:
mash, crash, dash,
trash, flash

Word Search Answers:

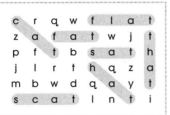

Page 33
A Fun Day!

Answers:
day, Ray, play,
bay, stay, gray

Word Search Answers:

Page 29
A Flat Hat!

Answers:
cat, fat, that, sat,
hat, Scat, flat

Word Search Answers:

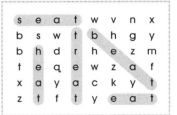

Page 34
Grandpa's Treat

Answers:
treat, eat, seat,
heat, beat

Word Search Answers:

Answer Key

Page 35

Three Lost Sheep

Answers:
sheep, steep, sleep, weep, beep, jeep

Word Search Answers:
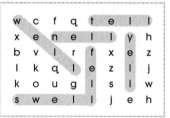

Page 40

Rice Is Nice!

Answers:
mice, slice, rice, price, nice

Word Search Answers:
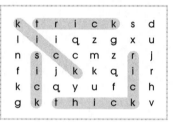

Page 36

In the Well

Answers:
Nell, well, yell, fell, Tell, swell

Word Search Answers:
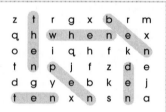

Page 41

A Sick Day

Answers:
Rick, thick, sick, kick, trick

Word Search Answers:
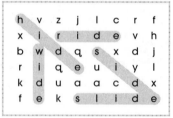

Page 37

A Letter From Ben

Answers:
den, pen, Then, when, Ben, ten

Word Search Answers:
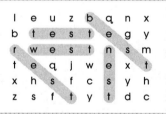

Page 42

Slide Down!

Answers:
ride, hide, slide, side, wide

Word Search Answers:
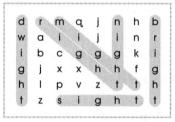

Page 38

The Best Nest

Answers:
west, best, nest, rest, test

Word Search Answers:
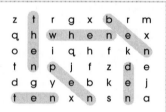

Page 43

The Night Sky

Answers:
Dwight, night, bright, might, sight, right

Word Search Answers:

Page 39

At the Vet

Answers:
Jet, get, vet, Let, bet, pet

Word Search Answers:
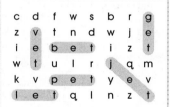

Page 44

A Pile of Leaves

Answers:
pile, dime, smile, time, while, lime

Word Search Answers:

Answer Key

Page 45
Jack and Jill

Answers:
Jill, hill, will,
fill, spill, till

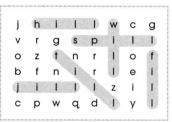
Word Search Answers:

Page 50
Did It Shrink?

Answers:
pink, sink, wink,
shrink, think

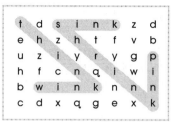
Word Search Answers:

Page 46
Can Tim Swim?

Answers:
Tim, swim, Kim,
him, slim

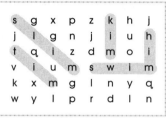
Word Search Answers:

Page 51
A Trip to China

Answers:
Kip, ship, tip,
slip, trip

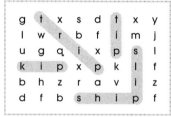
Word Search Answers:

Page 47
Twin Skaters

Answers:
twin, spin, skin,
win, grin

Word Search Answers:

Page 52
My Cat Kit

Answers:
Kit, bit, sit, fit, hit

Word Search Answers:

Page 48
Let's Dine!

Answers:
dine, pine, fine,
mine, nine

Word Search Answers:

Page 53
Tick-Tock

Answers:
block, knock, clock,
sock, tock

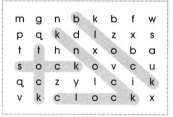
Word Search Answers:

Page 49
Spring

Answers:
spring, sing, bring,
thing, sting

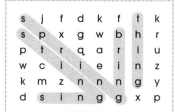
Word Search Answers:

Page 54
A Frog in a Log

Answers:
frog, jog, fog,
log, dog, hog

Word Search Answers:

Answer Key

Page 55
Smoke and Fire

Answers:
woke, smoke, choke, broke, spoke

Word Search Answers:

```
y r q c h o k e
z b f g t w j s
q r t w m q u p
j o s m o k e o
m k w d q k y k
x e c h l n e e
```

Page 56
Hop to It!

Answers:
mop, top, hop, shop, stop, chop

Word Search Answers:

```
t s f m l c r f
x t h k n l d h
b o q o c x f o
l p z e p m o p
c h o p u v z w
f q u m j t o p
```

Page 57
Down the Slope

Answers:
mope, Nope, rope, slope, hope

Word Search Answers:

```
c t s f r x h m
p g z l b o u l
w h b q o b p f
m o v k j p d q
k p d m o p e q
x e n o p e w c
```

Page 58
A Store for Hats

Answers:
store, more, wore, for, or, chore

Word Search Answers:

```
s q r p w j o u
h s z c f o r s
w x i h h f y t
z o k o d z w o
d e r r b k g r
x g x e m o r e
```

Page 59
Do Not Go!

Answers:
Dot, not, trot, got, hot, lot

Word Search Answers:

```
t r o t w g n x
b x w n k h o y
k h d r o q k t
t o q l w t x f
x t y o c d o t
z v f t y e b d
```

Page 60
A Parade Comes to Town

Answers:
town, clown, down, brown, gown, crown

Word Search Answers:

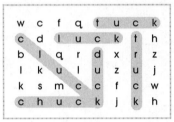

```
p d x c r o w n
g r t q l u e b
d o x o m o z g
o i w k w q w y
w o y n v n f n
n v b r o w n f
```

Page 61
Good Luck!

Answers:
Chuck, duck, cluck, truck, tuck, luck

Word Search Answers:

```
w c f q t u c k
c d l u c k t h
b l q r d x r z
l k u l u z u j
k s m c c f c w
c h u c k j k h
```

Page 62
Snug as a Bug

Answers:
bug, snug, plug, dug, rug

Word Search Answers:

```
z p r g x b r m
q l s n u g t x
o u t q h f k n
t g r j f z d e
d g y u b k u j
t e b u g s g a
```

Page 63
Jump Over!

Answers:
jump, stump, plump, thump, lump

Word Search Answers:

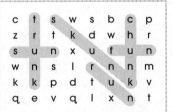

```
p e u z j q n x
l n g d q x g s
u u e z j n r t
m k m j w u x u
p h c p c s m m
z t h u m p d p
```

Page 64
Run Away!

Answers:
sun, fun, chunk, skunk, trunk, run

Word Search Answers:

```
c t s w s b c p
z r t k d w h r
s u n x u f u n
w n s l r n n m
k k p d t u k v
q e v q l x n t
```

Word Family: *ace* as in *race*

Look at the Word Bank.
Use the words to fill in the blanks.
Then read the story!

**Word
Bank**

pace

face

place

Grace

race

The Big Race

_____ is at the START line.

"I hope I win this _____!" she says.

Grace sees her dad's _____.

She smiles at him. Then the race begins.

Grace keeps up a fast _____.

"Go, Grace, go!" yells Dad.

Soon she is in first _____.

Look at the Word Bank.
Circle the words here.
Then read them!

n	p	n	q	v	z	b	w
x	a	p	e	f	m	x	s
b	c	i	l	h	a	v	a
t	e	k	z	a	c	c	u
r	a	c	e	c	c	y	e
x	g	r	a	c	e	e	u

Name _____   Date _____

Word Family: *ack* as in *sack*

Look at the Word Bank.
Use the words to fill in the blanks.
Then read the story!

Word Bank

sack

snack

back

Jack

quack

Quack! Quack!

Pat and _____ are at the lake.

They see the ducks swim _____ and forth.

They hear the ducks _____ at each other.

"I will feed them now," says Jack.

He puts his hand in the _____.

Now the ducks will have a good _____!

Look at the Word Bank.
Circle the words here.
Then read them!

b	j	b	a	c	k	s	d
l	x	a	q	z	g	n	u
n	s	p	c	c	z	a	j
f	a	j	v	k	q	c	r
k	c	q	u	a	c	k	g
g	k	l	d	c	o	z	v

Fill-in-the-Blank Stories: Word Families © 2008 by Linda B. Ross. Scholastic Teaching Resources.

Word Family: *ail* as in *pail*

Look at the Word Bank.
Use the words to fill in the blanks.
Then read the story!

Word Bank

pail

sail

Gail

tail

mail

Sail Away!

Dad showed the letter to _____.

"This came in the _____," Dad said.

"Uncle Jim wants us to _____ on his boat."

"Wow!" said Gail. "Can Spot come, too?"

"You bet!" said Dad. That made Spot happy.

He jumped on the _____ and wagged his

_____!

Word Search

Look at the Word Bank.
Circle the words here.
Then read them!

t	v	z	j	l	c	r	f
x	a	m	a	i	l	n	h
b	p	i	q	g	x	d	j
l	a	q	l	u	a	y	l
k	i	u	a	a	c	i	w
f	l	k	s	a	i	l	l

Name _____   Date _____

Look at the Word Bank.
Use the words to fill in the blanks.
Then read the story!

Word Bank

plane

rain

train

Jane

lane

A Train to Grandpa's House

_____ and her mom are on a _____.

They are going to visit Grandpa.

Jane looks out at the _____.

She thinks about Grandpa.

He lives in a pretty house on a _____.

Grandpa can do anything. He can even

fly a _____!

Look at the Word Bank.
Circle the words here.
Then read them!

j	t	x	i	o	b	h	b
p	a	g	u	j	v	c	t
l	z	n	r	a	i	n	r
a	k	n	e	j	q	e	a
n	d	p	e	v	z	s	i
e	h	l	a	n	e	y	n

Word Family: *ake* as in *cake*

Look at the Word Bank.
Use the words to fill in the blanks.
Then read the story!

Word Bank

take

wake

Jake

shake

cake

bake

Birthday Cake

"I will make a birthday _____ for Viv,"

said _____. "I will surprise her!"

Jake mixed the cake. Then he put it in the

oven to _____.

"Now I will _____ a nap," he said.

He fell fast asleep.

Then Jake felt someone _____ him.

"_____ up!" said Viv. "My cake is done!"

Word Search

Look at the Word Bank.
Circle the words here.
Then read them!

j	w	x	s	i	l	g	m
a	r	a	b	h	u	u	a
k	z	y	k	r	a	o	z
e	i	q	x	e	b	k	q
b	a	k	e	c	a	k	e
c	h	t	a	k	e	x	f

19

Word Family: *ale* as in *whale*

Look at the Word Bank.
Use the words to fill in the blanks.
Then read the story!

Word Bank

pale

sale

whale

tale

Dale

A Cap for Dale

Once there was a _____ named _____.

One day, Dale saw a man in a boat.

"Caps for _____!" said the man.

"Can I have a _____ blue cap?" asked Dale.

"Yes, you can!" said the man.

And that is the end of this _____!

Look at the Word Bank.
Circle the words here.
Then read them!

j	t	x	i	q	s	c	g
v	r	g	w	h	a	l	e
o	z	p	n	r	l	o	d
b	f	n	a	r	e	e	a
t	a	l	e	l	z	i	l
c	p	w	q	d	e	y	e

Fill-in-the-Blank Stories: Word Families © 2008 by Linda B. Ross. Scholastic Teaching Resources.

Word Family: *all* as in *ball*

Look at the Word Bank.
Use the words to fill in the blanks.
Then read the story!

Word Bank

all

ball

small

tall

wall

fall

A Fall Day

It was the first day of _____.

Tana looked at the _____ trees.

_____ the leaves were falling.

A _____ bird sat on a branch.

The sun looked like a big, yellow _____.

"I'm going to draw a picture," said Tana.

"Then Grandpa can hang it on the _____."

Look at the Word Bank.
Circle the words here.
Then read them!

s	g	x	p	o	a	h	p
j	m	g	n	j	l	u	w
t	q	a	z	d	l	o	f
v	a	u	l	r	q	e	a
k	i	l	e	l	n	y	l
w	a	l	l	b	a	l	l

Word Family: _am_ as in _jam_

Look at the Word Bank.
Use the words to fill in the blanks.
Then read the story!

Word Bank

jam

Pam

swam

am

Gram

Sam

I Am Sam

"Hi! My name is _____.

I _____ seven years old.

I have a little sister named _____.

I like to make peanut butter and _____

sandwiches. I also like to swim.

Last week, I _____ in a pool with

_____ and Gramps."

Word Search

Look at the Word Bank.
Circle the words here.
Then read them!

c	d	f	w	s	b	p	g
z	m	t	u	a	w	h	r
p	f	j	a	m	i	a	a
w	a	u	l	r	q	e	m
k	v	p	a	m	n	y	l
a	m	x	q	l	n	z	p

Word Family: *ame* as in *game*

Look at the Word Bank.
Use the words to fill in the blanks.
Then read the story!

Word Bank

game

name

shame

same

came

It's a Shame!

One day, my mom _____ home with a pup.

His _____ was Max.

Max and I like the _____ things.

We like to play catch.

It is our favorite _____.

I wish Max could go to school with me.

It's a _____ that he can't!

Word Search

Look at the Word Bank.
Circle the words here.
Then read them!

o	p	q	n	v	z	q	w
c	x	s	h	a	m	e	b
s	a	q	f	g	a	j	a
a	e	m	k	w	a	c	u
m	x	z	e	k	e	m	d
e	v	d	h	n	a	m	e

Word Family: _an_ as in _van_

Look at the Word Bank.
Use the words to fill in the blanks.
Then read the story!

Word Bank

can

pan

ran

tan

van

Dan

In the Van

Mom and Dad are packing the _____.

The family is going camping.

"_____ I help?" asked _____.

"Yes," said Mom. "Will you get the big _____?"

Dan _____ inside and got it.

"Now we can go!" said Dad.

The big _____ van drove off.

Word Search

Look at the Word Bank.
Circle the words here.
Then read them!

d	j	f	v	k	b	p	k
z	a	x	a	p	a	n	r
p	q	n	n	m	q	a	g
w	c	t	l	x	r	e	i
k	a	z	a	q	a	b	l
d	n	j	q	n	n	z	p

Word Family: *and* as in *hand*

Look at the Word Bank.
Use the words to fill in the blanks.
Then read the story!

Word Bank

stand

land

grand

hand

sand

band

A Grand Day

Tami took Dad's _____.

It was fun to walk in the soft _____.

They watched the seagulls take off and _____.

They listened to a _____ play music.

Then they had lunch at a hot dog _____.

It was a _____ day at the beach!

Word Search

Look at the Word Bank.
Circle the words here.
Then read them!

l	d	x	s	s	a	n	d
e	a	z	j	t	u	v	b
u	z	n	y	r	a	g	a
h	a	n	d	i	b	n	n
b	f	g	r	a	n	d	d
c	d	x	q	g	e	x	f

Word Family: ank as in **bank**

Look at the Word Bank.
Use the words to fill in the blanks.
Then read the story!

Word Bank

thank

blank

bank

drank

Hank

A Trip to the Bank

"Let's go to the _____," said _____.

"First drink your milk," said Grandma.

Hank _____ his milk. Then they left.

At the bank, Grandma and Hank met with a man.

Hank wrote his name in the _____ space.

Then the man gave Hank a bankbook.

" _____ you very much!" said Hank.

Word Search

Look at the Word Bank.
Circle the words here.
Then read them!

g	t	x	s	d	b	x	y
l	r	h	u	n	a	d	j
u	g	q	a	x	n	r	l
h	a	n	k	n	k	a	f
b	u	z	r	a	k	n	p
d	f	b	l	a	n	k	f

Name _____ Date _____

Word Family: *ap* as in *cap*

Look at the Word Bank.
Use the words to fill in the blanks.
Then read the story!

Word Bank

nap

yap

clap

lap

cap

snap

Snap and Clap

I put on my coat and _____.

I _____ my fingers and _____ my hands.

My pup comes running.

He starts to bark and _____.

He knows we are going for a walk.

When we get back, he will take a _____

on my _____.

Look at the Word Bank.
Circle the words here.
Then read them!

l	e	r	j	w	s	q	b
r	a	z	c	l	a	p	x
q	f	p	v	h	f	t	a
y	g	k	c	d	n	a	p
o	a	j	a	t	x	j	r
x	g	p	p	s	n	a	p

Name _____ Date _____

Word Family: *ash* as in *dash*

Look at the Word Bank.
Use the words to fill in the blanks.
Then read the story!

Word Bank

dash

flash

trash

crash

mash

Crash!

Sam was helping Aunt Jill _____ potatoes.

All of a sudden, they heard a _____ outside.

Aunt Jill was the first to _____ out the door.

Sam ran after her.

There was a raccoon in the _____ can.

"Go away!" yelled Aunt Jill and Sam.

The raccoon ran off in a _____!

Look at the Word Bank.
Circle the words here.
Then read them!

m	g	n	t	k	b	f	w
p	q	f	e	r	z	x	s
t	m	n	l	h	a	b	a
d	a	s	h	a	c	s	u
q	s	k	y	k	s	i	h
v	h	c	r	a	s	h	x

Name _____   Date _____

Word Family: *at* as in *cat*

Look at the Word Bank.
Use the words to fill in the blanks.
Then read the story!

Word Bank

hat

sat

cat

flat

fat

that

scat

A Flat Hat!

I have a pet _____.

He is big and _____.

Do you know what _____ cat did?

He _____ on Grandma's _____.

"_____, you silly cat," said Grandma.

"My hat is now _____!"

Word Search

Look at the Word Bank.
Circle the words here.
Then read them!

c	r	q	w	f	l	a	t
z	a	f	a	t	w	j	t
p	f	t	b	s	a	t	h
j	l	r	t	h	q	z	a
m	b	w	d	q	a	y	t
s	c	a	t	l	n	t	i

Word Family: *ate* as in *gate*

Look at the Word Bank.
Use the words to fill in the blanks.
Then read the story!

Word Bank

date

gate

hate

Kate

late

skate

A Date to Skate

_____ is my best friend.

We like to _____ together.

After school, we meet at the _____ to the park.

We are never _____ for our skating

_____.

We skate until five o'clock.

We _____ to stop, but it is time to go home.

Word Search

Look at the Word Bank.
Circle the words here.
Then read them!

b	c	v	g	r	m	d	s
l	a	t	e	a	b	u	k
d	g	e	b	k	t	j	a
z	a	q	z	a	f	e	t
k	c	t	m	t	c	x	e
h	a	t	e	e	k	z	v

Fill-in-the-Blank Stories: Word Families © 2008 by Linda B. Ross. Scholastic Teaching Resources.

Word Family: *ave* as in *cave*

Look at the Word Bank.
Use the words to fill in the blanks.
Then read the story!

Word Bank

gave

save

Dave

brave

cave

Brave Dave

One night, _____ had a dream.

He went into a _____ and saw a bear.

The bear's leg was stuck under a big rock.

"Can you _____ me?" asked the bear.

Dave pushed the rock away.

"You are a _____ boy!" said the bear.

Then he _____ Dave a big hug.

Word Search

Look at the Word Bank.
Circle the words here.
Then read them!

t	c	f	m	l	c	r	f
x	a	b	h	n	l	d	h
b	v	z	r	c	x	a	z
l	e	q	e	a	p	v	j
g	a	v	e	u	v	e	w
f	s	a	v	e	j	e	h

Word Family: *aw* as in *saw*; *awn* as in *dawn*

Look at the Word Bank.
Use the words to fill in the blanks.
Then read the story!

Word Bank

saw

draw

fawn

dawn

paw

lawn

A Fawn on the Lawn

My cat woke me up at _____.

He put his _____ on my hand.

We went to the window and _____

a _____.

It was standing on our _____!

It looked at us, and then ran away.

I want to _____ a picture of that fawn.

Word Search

Look at the Word Bank.
Circle the words here.
Then read them!

c	t	f	i	p	x	h	m
p	g	z	a	b	g	u	l
a	d	b	q	w	b	k	a
w	a	v	d	r	n	q	w
k	w	d	r	a	w	j	n
x	n	l	r	s	a	w	c

Word Family: *ay* as in *day*

Look at the Word Bank.
Use the words to fill in the blanks.
Then read the story!

Word Bank

bay

day

gray

play

Ray

stay

A Fun Day!

It was a sunny _____ at the beach.

"I like the beach!" said _____.

"I like to _____ in the sand and

swim in the _____!"

"What fun!" said Mom. "We can _____

until the sky turns _____!"

Word Search

Look at the Word Bank.
Circle the words here.
Then read them!

s	q	r	p	w	r	a	y
h	s	z	l	o	h	s	x
z	x	i	a	h	f	t	a
b	a	y	y	d	z	a	e
d	e	y	v	a	k	y	p
x	g	r	a	y	o	z	u

Name _____ Date _____

Look at the Word Bank.
Use the words to fill in the blanks.
Then read the story!

Word Bank

heat

beat

eat

treat

seat

Grandpa's Treat

Grandpa is making a special _____.

It is something good to _____.

I come to the table and take my _____.

Something is baking. I can feel the _____.

Grandpa brings out his apple pie.

It's the best! It can't be _____!

Look at the Word Bank.
Circle the words here.
Then read them!

s	e	a	t	w	v	n	x
b	s	w	t	b	h	g	y
b	h	d	r	h	e	z	m
t	e	q	e	w	z	a	f
x	a	y	a	c	k	y	t
z	t	f	t	y	e	a	t

Word Family: *eep* as in *jeep*

Look at the Word Bank.
Use the words to fill in the blanks.
Then read the story!

Word Bank

beep

weep

sheep

jeep

sleep

steep

Three Lost Sheep

Three _____ went for a walk.

They climbed a _____ hill and ate grass.

Then they were tired. So they went to _____.

It was dark when they woke up.

They were scared and began to _____.

Then the sheep heard a sound. _____!

It was their pals in a _____!

Word Search

Look at the Word Bank.
Circle the words here.
Then read them!

p	d	x	s	l	e	e	p
j	r	b	q	h	u	u	b
w	e	x	e	a	e	z	g
e	i	e	k	e	i	e	y
e	o	y	p	v	p	w	p
p	v	s	t	e	e	p	f

Word Family: *ell* as in **well**

Look at the Word Bank.
Use the words to fill in the blanks.
Then read the story!

Word Bank

swell

fell

tell

Nell

well

yell

In the Well

_____ needed some water.

So she went to the _____.

Then Nell heard a loud _____.

"Help! I _____ in the well," said Sam.

"_____ me what to do."

"Jump in the pail," said Nell. "I will pull you up."

"You are a _____ pal!" said Sam.

Word Search

Look at the Word Bank.
Circle the words here.
Then read them!

w	c	f	q	t	e	l	l
x	e	n	e	l	l	y	h
b	v	l	r	f	x	e	z
l	k	q	l	e	z	l	j
k	o	u	g	l	s	l	w
s	w	e	l	l	j	e	h

Word Family: *en* as in *pen*

Look at the Word Bank.
Use the words to fill in the blanks.
Then read the story!

Word Bank

then

ten

pen

Ben

den

when

A Letter From Ben

Ben sat in his _____.

He picked up his _____.

"I'll write to Manny," he said.

Manny used to live next door.

_____ Manny moved away.

Ben was sad _____ he left.

But next summer, Manny will visit _____.

They will spend _____ days together!

Word Search

Look at the Word Bank.
Circle the words here.
Then read them!

z	t	r	g	x	b	r	m
q	h	w	h	e	n	e	x
o	e	i	q	h	f	k	n
t	n	p	j	f	z	d	e
d	g	y	e	b	k	e	j
t	e	n	x	n	s	n	a

Name _____   Date _____

Look at the Word Bank.
Use the words to fill in the blanks.
Then read the story!

Word Bank

rest

best

test

nest

west

The Best Nest

Mama Bird flew east and _____.

She looked for the _____ tree in which

to build her _____.

Soon her nest was filled with babies!

"You must eat and _____," said Mama Bird.

"Then you will _____ your wings

and fly away."

Word Search

Look at the Word Bank.
Circle the words here.
Then read them!

l	e	u	z	b	q	n	x
b	t	e	s	t	e	g	y
r	w	e	s	t	n	s	m
t	e	q	j	w	e	x	t
x	h	s	f	c	s	y	h
z	s	f	t	y	t	d	c

Fill-in-the-Blank Stories: Word Families © 2008 by Linda B. Ross. Scholastic Teaching Resources.

Name _____   Date _____

Word Family: *et* as in *pet*

Look at the Word Bank.
Use the words to fill in the blanks.
Then read the story!

Word Bank
bet
pet
get
Jet
let
vet

At the Vet

Dennis has a dog named _____.

It was time for Jet to _____ a checkup.

So they went to the _____.

"_____ me take a look at him," said the vet.

"Is Jet okay?" asked Dennis.

"You _____ !" said the vet.

"He's a fine _____!"

Word Search

Look at the Word Bank.
Circle the words here.
Then read them!

c	d	f	w	s	b	r	g
z	v	t	n	d	w	j	e
i	e	b	e	t	i	z	t
w	t	u	l	r	j	q	m
k	v	p	e	t	y	e	v
l	e	t	q	l	n	z	t

Word Family: *ice* as in **nice**

Look at the Word Bank.
Use the words to fill in the blanks.
Then read the story!

Word Bank

nice

price

slice

mice

rice

Rice Is Nice!

Once there were three _____.

Each week, the mice bought a _____ of cheese.

One day while shopping, they saw a bowl

of _____.

"How much is the rice?" asked the mice.

"The _____ is 50 cents," said Hen.

"We'll take it," they said.

"Rice will make a _____ meal!"

Look at the Word Bank.
Circle the words here.
Then read them!

d	n	f	j	v	z	b	p
x	i	q	k	r	m	x	r
b	c	i	m	h	g	v	i
t	e	k	z	i	l	w	c
r	i	c	e	b	c	y	e
x	s	l	i	c	e	e	u

Fill-in-the-Blank Stories: Word Families © 2008 by Linda B. Ross. Scholastic Teaching Resources.

Word Family: *ick* as in *kick*

Look at the Word Bank.
Use the words to fill in the blanks.
Then read the story!

Word Bank

kick

trick

thick

Rick

sick

A Sick Day

_____ was in bed with a bad cold.

He lay under a _____ blanket.

"I don't like being _____," said Rick.

"I want to play soccer. I want to _____

the ball and make a goal!"

"Soon you will do that," said Mom.

"But for now, this hot soup should do the _____!"

Look at the Word Bank.
Circle the words here.
Then read them!

k	t	r	i	c	k	s	d
l	i	i	q	z	g	x	u
n	s	c	c	m	z	r	j
f	i	j	k	k	q	i	r
k	c	q	y	u	f	c	h
g	k	t	h	i	c	k	v

Word Family: *ide* as in *ride*

Look at the Word Bank.
Use the words to fill in the blanks.
Then read the story!

Slide Down!

Word Bank

wide

hide

slide

ride

side

Penny and Pilar are good friends.

They _____ their bikes together.

They play _____-and-seek together.

One day, Penny said, "Let's go down the

_____ together!"

So they sat _____ by side, but then they got stuck.

"This slide isn't _____ enough for two!" said Pilar.

Word Search

Look at the Word Bank.
Circle the words here.
Then read them!

h	v	z	j	l	c	r	f
x	i	r	i	d	e	v	h
b	w	d	q	s	x	d	j
r	i	q	e	u	i	y	l
k	d	u	a	a	c	d	x
f	e	k	s	l	i	d	e

Name _____ Date _____

Word Family: *ight* as in *night*

Look at the Word Bank.
Use the words to fill in the blanks.
Then read the story!

Word Bank

bright

right

Dwight

sight

night

might

The Night Sky

_____ got a telescope for his birthday.

Each _____, he looks at the sky.

He likes the _____ moon and twinkling stars.

Someday he _____ even see a shooting star.

What a pretty _____ that would be!

A telescope was the _____ gift for Dwight.

Word Search

Look at the Word Bank.
Circle the words here.
Then read them!

d	r	m	q	j	n	h	b
w	a	i	i	j	i	n	r
i	b	c	g	g	g	k	i
g	j	x	x	h	h	f	g
h	l	p	v	z	t	t	h
t	z	s	i	g	h	t	t

Word Family: *ile* as in *smile*; *ime* as in *dime*

Look at the Word Bank.
Use the words to fill in the blanks.
Then read the story!

Word Bank

smile

while

pile

dime

lime

time

A Pile of Leaves

"Look at that _____ of leaves," said Grandma

to Marcos.

"I'll pay you a _____ for each bag you rake."

Marcos had a big _____ on his face.

"I have _____ to do that job!" he said.

Grandma baked _____ Marcos raked.

She wanted to surprise him with a _____ pie.

Word Search

Look at the Word Bank.
Circle the words here.
Then read them!

l	d	x	s	i	l	g	m
i	v	i	b	m	u	u	a
m	z	y	m	n	i	o	z
e	i	q	x	e	b	l	q
t	i	m	e	p	i	l	e
c	w	h	i	l	e	x	f

Name _____ Date _____

Word Family: *ill* as in *hill*

Look at the Word Bank.
Use the words to fill in the blanks.
Then read the story!

Word Bank

will

spill

Jill

till

hill

fill

Jack and Jill

Jack and _____ needed water.

The well was at the top of the _____.

"We _____ climb the hill," said Jill.

"We will _____ our pails," said Jack.

Then Jack and Jill came down the hill.

"Be careful not to _____ the water," said Jill.

"It must last _____ tomorrow."

Word Search

Look at the Word Bank.
Circle the words here.
Then read them!

j	h	i	l	l	w	c	g
v	r	g	s	p	i	l	l
o	z	t	n	r	l	o	f
b	f	n	i	r	l	e	i
j	i	l	l	l	z	i	l
c	p	w	q	d	l	y	l

Name _____   Date _____

Look at the Word Bank.
Use the words to fill in the blanks.
Then read the story!

Word Bank

slim

him

Tim

Kim

swim

Can Tim Swim?

_____ is six years old.

He wanted to learn how to _____.

So he asked Aunt _____ to teach

_____.

Aunt Kim is tall and _____.

She is a good swimmer.

Now Tim and Aunt Kim swim together!

Word Search

Look at the Word Bank.
Circle the words here.
Then read them!

s	g	x	p	z	k	h	j
j	l	g	n	j	i	u	h
t	q	i	z	d	m	o	i
v	i	u	m	s	w	i	m
k	x	m	g	l	n	y	q
w	y	l	p	r	d	l	n

Name _____   Date _____

Look at the Word Bank.
Use the words to fill in the blanks.
Then read the story!

Word Bank

grin

spin

win

twin

skin

Twin Skaters

Lana and her _____ sister like to skate.

Look at Lana and Lola _____ and twirl!

Sometimes they fall down and _____

their knees.

But they get up and keep skating.

Will the twins _____ first prize?

Yes! Look at them _____ with joy!

Look at the Word Bank.
Circle the words here.
Then read them!

c	d	f	w	s	b	p	g
z	m	t	i	j	p	h	r
t	w	i	n	m	v	i	i
w	a	u	l	r	q	e	n
k	v	s	k	i	n	y	l
a	c	x	q	l	k	z	p

Word Family: *ine* as in *nine*

Look at the Word Bank.
Use the words to fill in the blanks.
Then read the story!

Word Bank

nine

pine

fine

dine

mine

Let's Dine!

"Would you like to _____ with me?" Sammy

asked Suki.

"My house is in that big _____ tree."

"What a _____ house," said Suki.

"Yes, it is all _____!" said Sammy proudly.

Sammy and Suki had a good dinner.

They shared _____ delicious nuts.

Look at the Word Bank.
Circle the words here.
Then read them!

o	p	q	n	v	z	q	w
d	x	v	p	i	n	e	b
n	i	q	f	f	a	j	a
i	e	n	k	w	i	c	u
n	x	z	e	k	r	n	d
e	v	d	h	m	i	n	e

Name _____ Date _____

Look at the Word Bank.
Use the words to fill in the blanks.
Then read the story!

Word Bank

thing

sing

sting

bring

spring

Spring

My favorite season is _____.

I like the birds that _____ outside my window.

I like having picnics with my family.

We _____ lots of good food to eat.

Flowers are another _____ I like.

But the bees are no fun—they _____!

Word Search

Look at the Word Bank.
Circle the words here.
Then read them!

s	j	f	d	k	f	t	k
s	p	x	g	w	b	h	r
p	t	r	q	a	r	i	u
w	c	i	i	e	i	n	z
k	m	z	n	n	n	g	y
d	s	i	n	g	g	x	p

Name _____   Date _____

Word Family: *ink* as in *sink*

Look at the Word Bank.
Use the words to fill in the blanks.
Then read the story!

Did It Shrink?

Word Bank

think

pink

sink

shrink

wink

Betty's _____ T-shirt was dirty.

"I'll wash it in the _____," she said.

Quick as a _____, she washed the shirt.

Then she looked at it.

"Did my T-shirt _____?" she asked.

"I _____ it did! I'll have to give it to my

little sister!"

Look at the Word Bank.
Circle the words here.
Then read them!

t	d	s	i	n	k	z	d
e	h	z	h	t	f	v	b
u	z	i	y	r	y	g	p
h	f	c	n	q	i	w	i
b	w	i	n	k	n	n	n
c	d	x	q	g	e	x	k

Fill-in-the-Blank Stories: Word Families © 2008 by Linda B. Ross. Scholastic Teaching Resources.

Word Family: *ip* as in *ship*

Look at the Word Bank.
Use the words to fill in the blanks.
Then read the story!

Word Bank
ship
trip
slip
Kip
tip

A Trip to China

_____ and Dad were at the dock.

They were saying good-bye to Grandpa.

He was sailing to China on a big _____.

They saw Grandpa _____ his hat.

That was his way of saying good-bye.

Soon the ship began to _____ away.

"Have a good _____!" called Dad and Kip.

Word Search

Look at the Word Bank.
Circle the words here.
Then read them!

g	t	x	s	d	t	x	y
l	w	r	b	f	i	m	j
u	g	q	i	x	p	s	l
k	i	p	x	p	k	l	f
b	h	z	r	a	v	i	z
d	f	b	s	h	i	p	f

Word Family: *it* as in *sit*

Look at the Word Bank.
Use the words to fill in the blanks.
Then read the story!

Word Bank

hit

bit

Kit

fit

sit

My Cat Kit

I have a cat named _____.

She may be a _____ small, but she is

growing fast!

Kit likes to _____ with me when I read.

She can _____ on my lap.

She likes to _____ the book with her little paw.

How cute is that?

Word Search

Look at the Word Bank.
Circle the words here.
Then read them!

l	e	r	j	b	s	q	b
r	k	z	x	i	q	p	x
q	f	p	v	t	d	t	g
h	g	m	k	d	f	i	t
r	i	j	i	x	y	j	r
x	q	t	t	s	i	t	p

Word Family: *ock* as in *clock*

Look at the Word Bank.
Use the words to fill in the blanks.
Then read the story!

Tick-Tock

Leon put another _____ on his house.

Then he heard Mom _____ at the door.

"It's time for bed," she said.

Leon looked at the _____ .

He took off each _____ and got into bed.

"I'll finish my house tomorrow," he said.

"Tick-_____," went the clock. Soon Leon was

fast asleep.

Word Bank

sock

knock

clock

block

tock

Word Search

Look at the Word Bank.
Circle the words here.
Then read them!

m	g	n	b	k	b	f	w
p	q	k	d	l	z	x	s
t	t	h	n	x	o	b	a
s	o	c	k	o	v	c	u
q	c	z	y	l	c	i	k
v	k	c	l	o	c	k	x

Word Family: *og* as in *log*

Look at the Word Bank.
Use the words to fill in the blanks.
Then read the story!

Word Bank

dog

fog

hog

jog

log

frog

A Frog in a Log

One day a little green _____ went out

to _____.

"There is too much _____," said Frog.

"It is hard to see."

So Frog went inside a _____ to take a nap.

Soon he heard a _____ bark and

a _____ oink.

"The fog is gone," they said. "Come out and play!"

Word Search

Look at the Word Bank.
Circle the words here.
Then read them!

b	u	v	j	r	m	d	s
d	o	g	e	o	b	u	k
f	q	e	k	l	g	j	f
z	o	q	z	o	p	v	r
h	o	g	m	g	l	x	o
p	q	y	c	e	k	z	g

Word Family: _oke_ as in _broke_

Look at the Word Bank.
Use the words to fill in the blanks.
Then read the story!

Word Bank

broke

spoke

smoke

woke

choke

Smoke and Fire

One morning, Pilar _____ up early.

Her house was filled with _____.

Poor Pilar began to cough and _____!

The firefighters came and _____ down the door.

Then they put out the fire.

Later on, Pilar _____ to them.

"You saved my life!" she said. "Thank you!"

Word Search

Look at the Word Bank.
Circle the words here.
Then read them!

y	r	q	c	h	o	k	e
z	b	f	g	t	w	j	s
q	r	t	w	m	q	u	p
j	o	s	m	o	k	e	o
m	k	w	d	q	k	y	k
x	e	c	h	l	n	e	e

Word Family: *op* as in *mop*

Look at the Word Bank.
Use the words to fill in the blanks.
Then read the story!

Word Bank

chop

top

stop

mop

shop

hop

Hop to It!

Rudy got the _____ and cleaned his

house from _____ to bottom.

"Now I must _____ to the market and

_____ for food," he said.

Rudy came home and didn't _____ working.

"Now I must _____ the food," he said.

Rudy was having a party!

Word Search

Look at the Word Bank.
Circle the words here.
Then read them!

t	s	f	m	l	c	r	f
x	t	h	k	n	l	d	h
b	o	q	o	c	x	f	o
l	p	z	e	p	m	o	p
c	h	o	p	u	v	z	w
f	q	u	m	j	t	o	p

Fill-in-the-Blank Stories: Word Families © 2008 by Linda B. Ross. Scholastic Teaching Resources.

Word Family: *ope* as in *rope*

Look at the Word Bank.
Use the words to fill in the blanks.
Then read the story!

Word Bank

hope

mope

nope

rope

slope

Down the Slope

"It isn't good to _____," said Chip to Kip.

"Let's play in the snow."

"_____," said Kip. "It's too cold."

Chip tied a _____ to his sled.

"Come on," he said. "I'll pull you down

the _____."

Kip went down the slope. "Whee!" he said.

"I _____ you're having fun!" said Chip.

Word Search

Look at the Word Bank.
Circle the words here.
Then read them!

c	t	s	f	r	x	h	m
p	g	z	l	b	o	u	l
w	h	b	q	o	b	p	f
m	o	v	k	j	p	q	e
k	p	d	m	o	p	e	q
x	e	n	o	p	e	w	c

Name _____ Date _____

Look at the Word Bank.
Use the words to fill in the blanks.
Then read the story!

A Store for Hats

Millie went to the _____.

She tried on _____ than fifty hats!

She looked closely at each hat she _____.

"Is this hat _____ me?" she asked.

"Should I get a red hat _____ a blue one?"

At last Millie chose a hat.

"Buying a hat is a _____!" she said.

Word Bank

or

for

wore

chore

more

store

Word Search

Look at the Word Bank.
Circle the words here.
Then read them!

s	q	r	p	w	j	o	u
h	s	z	c	f	o	r	s
w	x	i	h	h	f	y	t
z	o	k	o	d	z	w	o
d	e	r	r	b	k	g	r
x	g	x	e	m	o	r	e

Word Family: *ot* as in *hot*

Look at the Word Bank.
Use the words to fill in the blanks.
Then read the story!

Do Not Go!

_____ was a good horse.

But she was getting old.

She could _____ pull heavy loads.

She could not _____ very fast.

She _____ tired on _____ days.

"Should I go?" she asked Farmer Joe.

"No!" he said. "I'd miss you a _____!"

Word Bank

lot

not

Dot

trot

hot

got

Word Search

Look at the Word Bank.
Circle the words here.
Then read them!

t	r	o	t	w	g	n	x
b	x	w	n	k	h	o	y
k	h	d	r	o	q	k	t
t	o	q	l	w	t	x	f
x	t	y	o	c	d	o	t
z	v	f	t	y	e	b	d

Name _____   Date _____

Look at the Word Bank.
Use the words to fill in the blanks.
Then read the story!

Word Bank

down

gown

town

brown

clown

crown

A Parade Comes to Town

There was a parade in our _____.

I saw a funny _____ jump up and

_____.

He wore _____ shoes on his big feet.

I saw a lady in a beautiful _____.

She wore a gold _____ on her head and

waved to us. Parades are fun!

Look at the Word Bank.
Circle the words here.
Then read them!

p	d	x	c	r	o	w	n
g	r	t	q	l	u	e	b
d	o	x	o	m	o	z	g
o	i	w	k	w	q	w	y
w	o	y	n	v	n	f	n
n	v	b	r	o	w	n	f

Word Family: *uck* as in *duck*

Look at the Word Bank.
Use the words to fill in the blanks.
Then read the story!

**Word
Bank**

luck

truck

tuck

cluck

duck

Chuck

Good Luck!

_____ has many toys.

He has a _____ that can quack.

He has a hen that can _____.

He also has a big, red _____.

One night, Grandma came to _____ him in.

Chuck's toys were in his bed.

"Good _____ sleeping with all that stuff!"

Grandma said.

Word Search

Look at the Word Bank.
Circle the words here.
Then read them!

w	c	f	q	t	u	c	k
c	d	l	u	c	k	t	h
b	l	q	r	d	x	r	z
l	k	u	l	u	z	u	j
k	s	m	c	c	f	c	w
c	h	u	c	k	j	k	h

Word Family: *ug* as in *rug*

Look at the Word Bank.
Use the words to fill in the blanks.
Then read the story!

Word Bank
rug
snug
plug
bug
dug

Snug as a Bug

A _____ was _____ in her bed.

Then a dog barked and woke her up.

"I'll _____ my ears," she said.

But that didn't help.

So she _____ a deep hole and crawled in.

Then she put a _____ over the hole.

"Now I can sleep!" said the bug.

Word Search

Look at the Word Bank.
Circle the words here.
Then read them!

z	p	r	g	x	b	r	m
q	l	s	n	u	g	t	x
o	u	t	q	h	f	k	n
t	g	r	j	f	z	d	e
d	g	y	u	b	k	u	j
t	e	b	u	g	s	g	a

Word Family: *ump* as in *jump*

Look at the Word Bank.
Use the words to fill in the blanks.
Then read the story!

Word Bank

lump

stump

thump

jump

plump

Jump Over!

"Let's _____ over the tree

_____," said Squirrel. "It will be fun!"

Squirrel jumped. Then it was Bear's turn.

But Bear was too _____ to jump.

He landed on the ground with a big _____!

"Oh my! I have a _____ on my head,"

said Bear. "Let's play another game!"

Word Search

Look at the Word Bank.
Circle the words here.
Then read them!

p	e	u	z	j	q	n	x
l	n	g	d	q	x	g	s
u	u	e	z	j	n	r	t
m	k	m	j	w	u	x	u
p	h	c	p	c	s	m	m
z	t	h	u	m	p	d	p

Name _____ Date _____

Word Family: *un* as in *fun*; *unk* as in *trunk*

Look at the Word Bank.
Use the words to fill in the blanks.
Then read the story!

Word Bank

fun

run

sun

trunk

skunk

chunk

Run Away!

It was a pretty day. The _____ was out.

Chip and Kip were having _____.

They were eating a big _____ of

watermelon.

All of a sudden, they saw a _____!

It came out of the tree _____.

"Let's _____!" said Chip to Kip.

Word Search

Look at the Word Bank.
Circle the words here.
Then read them!

c	t	s	w	s	b	c	p
z	r	t	k	d	w	h	r
s	u	n	x	u	f	u	n
w	n	s	l	r	n	n	m
k	k	p	d	t	u	k	v
q	e	v	q	l	x	n	t

SCHOLASTIC

From the Editors at Scholastic Teaching Resources

Dear Reader,

We're always delighted when teachers say, "Your books are the ones we use . . . the ones that go to school with us for a day's work . . . the ones that go home with us to help in planning. . . ."

Your comments tell us that our books work for you—supporting you in your daily planning and long-range goals, helping you bring fresh ideas into your classroom, and keeping you up to date with the latest trends in education. In fact, many Scholastic Teaching Resources are written by teachers, like you, who work in schools every day.

If through your teaching you have developed materials that you believe would help other PreK–8 teachers—help save them time, help engage their students, help enliven or enrich their teaching—please let us know! Send us a letter that includes your name, address, phone number, and the grade you teach; a table of contents for your book idea; and a sample chapter or activities to:

> Manuscript Editor
> Scholastic Teaching Resources
> 557 Broadway
> New York, NY 10012

Please understand that because of the large volume of interesting teacher ideas we receive, it will take several months before you hear from us.

Many thanks for all the work you do for children!

—The Editors

Teaching *Resources*

Fill-in-the-Blank Stories

WORD FAMILIES

Short, simple, and engaging, these cloze stories give children the repeated practice they need to master words belonging to 50 different word families. Children use a word bank and text and picture clues to fill in missing words that give each story meaning. A word search provides further practice in reading and spelling target words. Great for independent learning or homework.

Other Books by This Author:

Fill-in-the-Blank Stories:
Sight Words
Grades K–2
ISBN: 0-439-55431-4

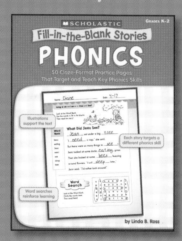

Fill-in-the-Blank Stories:
Phonics
Grades K–2
ISBN: 0-439-45863-3

The Big Book of
Pocket Chart Poems:
ABCs & 123s
Grades PreK–1
ISBN: 0-439-51385-5

$11.99 U.S.

ISBN-13: 978-0-439-45861-0
ISBN-10: 0-439-45861-7

51199

EAN

9 780439 458610

www.scholastic.com

HATS

Hooked on Crochet!™

16
*Fun Crochet
Hat Designs!*

878545